BEYOND THE LOOKING GLASS:

Adventures in a Digital World

BY JENNY JAY

INTERODUCTION

Welcome to a realm where reality and imagination intertwine, and the boundaries of the physical world dissolve into a digital tapestry of endless possibilities. In this extraordinary landscape, the title "Beyond the Looking Glass: Adventures in a Digital World" beckons us to embark on a transformative journey through the wonders of technology, innovation, and human creativity.

In the digital age, we find ourselves immersed in a realm that transcends the confines of traditional reality. From the mesmerizing depths of Virtual Reality to the captivating interplay of Augmented Reality, this digital world invites us to explore uncharted territories and experience the extraordinary without leaving the comfort of our surroundings.

The looking glass, once a mere portal to another world in literature, has now become the gateway to a multifaceted digital universe. Within its realm, we encounter AI-powered creations that mirror human intelligence, breathtaking digital artworks that challenge our perception, and interactive experiences that blur the lines between creator and audience.

"Beyond the Looking Glass: Adventures in a Digital World" serves as an invitation to step outside the ordinary and venture into an alternate dimension where creativity knows no bounds. It is a celebration of human ingenuity, where technology amplifies artistic expression, and innovation propels us to new heights of human potential.

Throughout this exploration, we will encounter visionary artists, trailblazing technologists, and pioneers of the digital landscape. We will delve into the impact of Augmented Reality on industries like education and healthcare, uncover the transformative power of Virtual Reality in storytelling and gaming, and examine the ethical considerations that arise in this ever-evolving digital frontier.

So, join us on this exhilarating expedition as we traverse the looking glass into a world where reality meets imagination, and the possibilities are as boundless as our dreams. Together, we will navigate the digital wonders, seek inspiration in the fusion of art and technology, and embrace the excitement of endless adventures in the captivating realm of "Beyond the Looking Glass: Adventures in a Digital World."

CHAPTER ONE

The Digital Frontier: Exploring New Horizons in a Hyperconnected World

In the 21st century, we find ourselves standing at the precipice of a digital frontier that is transforming the very fabric of human existence. The convergence of technology and connectivity has given birth to a digital landscape brimming with possibilities and potential. This realm, often referred to as the "Digital Frontier," offers us unprecedented opportunities to explore, create, and connect like never before. In this article, we shall embark on a journey to understand the significance of the Digital Frontier and the impact it has on our lives.

Defining the Digital Frontier:

The Digital Frontier represents the uncharted territory of the digital realm, encompassing various technologies and their profound influence on society. It is a landscape characterized by virtual reality, augmented reality, artificial intelligence, cryptocurrency, social media, and the Internet of Things (IoT). This digital ecosystem continues to expand and evolve, reshaping the way we interact, learn, work, and communicate.

The Advent of Virtual Reality and Augmented Reality:

Virtual Reality (VR) and Augmented Reality (AR) are two technological marvels that have brought about a paradigm shift in how we experience the world. VR immerses users in computer-generated environments, providing a sense of presence in a simulated reality. On the other hand, AR overlays digital information onto the physical world, enhancing our perception and interaction with reality.

From immersive gaming experiences to virtual travel, VR opens up a world of possibilities, while AR finds applications in fields like medicine, education, and industrial training. These technologies have the power to transform how we learn, entertain ourselves, and visualize information.

Artificial Intelligence: The Brainpower Behind the Scenes:

Artificial Intelligence (AI) is the driving force behind many of the advancements on the Digital Frontier. AI systems possess the ability to learn, reason, and make decisions, often surpassing human capabilities in specific tasks. From voice assistants like Siri and Alexa to advanced AI algorithms powering recommendation systems and autonomous vehicles, AI is an omnipresent force shaping our daily lives.

However, as AI becomes more integrated into society, it raises questions about ethics, privacy, and the potential for job displacement. Striking a balance between the benefits of AI and its responsible use remains a crucial challenge.

Cryptocurrency and Blockchain: Redefining Finance and Security:

Cryptocurrency and blockchain technology have emerged as disruptive elements on the Digital Frontier. Cryptocurrencies like Bitcoin and Ethereum offer decentralized and secure alternatives to traditional financial systems. Blockchain, the underlying technology behind cryptocurrencies, ensures transparency and immutability in data management.

As financial institutions explore the potential of blockchain, its applications extend beyond finance to areas like supply chain management, healthcare, and voting systems. Nonetheless, regulatory challenges and environmental concerns related to cryptocurrency mining warrant careful consideration.

Social Media: The Global Village at Our Fingertips:

Social media platforms have become the backbone of digital connectivity, enabling individuals to connect, share, and express themselves on a global scale. They have revolutionized communication, breaking barriers of distance and time. Social media has facilitated social movements, influenced public opinion, and allowed businesses to reach their target audiences with precision.

However, the impact of social media isn't without its drawbacks. Concerns about privacy, fake news, cyberbullying, and the addictive nature of these platforms call for a mindful approach to digital engagement.

Navigating the Digital Frontier:

As we venture further into the Digital Frontier, it is essential to navigate this new territory responsibly and ethically. Embracing technological advancements while being aware of their potential consequences empowers us to harness the true potential of the digital realm.

Digital Literacy: Developing digital literacy and critical thinking skills is crucial to discern reliable information from misinformation and to protect oneself from cyber threats.

Data Privacy and Security: Safeguarding personal data and maintaining digital privacy should be a priority, both for individuals and organizations.

Ethical Use of Technology: Embracing technology with ethical considerations will ensure that we use

AI, VR, AR, and other innovations for the greater good and not at the expense of human values.

The Digital Frontier beckons us with an array of opportunities and challenges. Embracing the transformative power of technology while remaining conscious of its potential ramifications will enable us to embark on a journey of progress and discovery in this hyperconnected world. As pioneers on this Digital Frontier, let us explore with curiosity, create with purpose, and build a future that harnesses the full potential of the digital age for the betterment of humanity.

Exploring the Digital World: A Transformative Journey Impacting Society

In the past few decades, humanity has witnessed an unprecedented transformation brought about by the advent of the digital world. This digital revolution has permeated every aspect of our lives, reshaping how we communicate, work, learn, and even perceive reality. The concept of the digital world refers to the interconnected network of information, technologies, and virtual spaces that have become an integral part of modern society. In this article, we will delve into the essence of the digital world and examine its profound impact on society.

Understanding the Digital World:

The digital world is a vast ecosystem that revolves around the Internet and digital technologies. At its core lies the Internet, a global network that connects billions of devices, enabling the exchange of information, ideas, and services in real-time. This interconnectedness has given rise to a digital landscape where geographical boundaries blur, and distances become virtually insignificant.

In this realm, data flows seamlessly, and communication transcends traditional constraints. Social media platforms enable us to connect with friends and family across continents instantly. Online marketplaces allow us to shop from international vendors at the click of a button. Educational institutions offer e-learning opportunities accessible to students worldwide. The digital world has created an interconnected web of possibilities, enhancing the quality of life and expanding the horizons of human potential.

The Digital Transformation of Industries:

The impact of the digital world extends beyond our personal lives; it has dramatically transformed industries and economies. Businesses are embracing digital technologies to streamline operations, improve efficiency, and reach wider audiences. E-commerce has revolutionized retail, empowering consumers with convenience and choice. Traditional media has evolved into digital media, providing instant news updates and personalized content.

Moreover, the digital world has given rise to disruptive innovations like Artificial Intelligence (AI), Internet of Things (IoT), and blockchain, opening up new realms of possibilities in fields such as healthcare, finance, transportation, and manufacturing. These technologies are driving automation, optimizing processes, and accelerating scientific breakthroughs.

Challenges and Concerns:

While the digital world has undoubtedly presented us with numerous opportunities, it also brings with it several challenges and concerns. One of the most pressing issues is data privacy and security. With vast amounts of data being generated and shared every day, protecting sensitive information has become a critical priority. Cyberattacks and data breaches pose a threat to individuals, businesses, and even governments.

Additionally, the digital world has given rise to the issue of digital divide - the gap between those who have access to digital technologies and those who do not. This disparity can further exacerbate existing social and economic inequalities. Ensuring equitable access to digital resources is essential to promote inclusivity and bridge the digital divide.

Cultivating Digital Literacy and Responsibility:

As the digital world continues to evolve, it is imperative for individuals and societies to cultivate digital literacy and responsibility. Digital literacy encompasses the ability to navigate and evaluate information online critically. Understanding concepts such as fake news, misinformation, and digital etiquette are essential components of digital literacy.

Furthermore, digital responsibility entails using technology ethically, respecting others' privacy, and being mindful of the impact of our digital actions. Responsible use of social media, safe online practices, and conscious consumption of digital content are vital aspects of being responsible digital citizens.

Embracing the Digital Future:

The digital world has undoubtedly ushered in an era of unprecedented progress and innovation. However, its impact on society also comes with the responsibility to navigate the digital landscape wisely. Embracing the digital future requires striking a balance between the benefits of technology and the preservation of human values.

By harnessing the potential of the digital world for positive change, we can empower ourselves to address global challenges, foster meaningful connections, and create a better world for future generations. As we continue our journey into the digital age, let us embrace the digital world with optimism, curiosity, and a commitment to using its transformative power for the greater good.

A Historical Perspective on the Evolution of Technology and its Role in Shaping the Digital Landscape

The history of technology is a tale of human ingenuity and innovation that spans millennia. From the invention of the wheel to the age of the internet, technological advancements have shaped the course of human civilization, constantly propelling us towards new frontiers. In this article, we embark on a journey through time to explore the historical evolution of technology and its pivotal role in shaping the digital landscape we inhabit today.

The Birth of Technology: From Ancient Ingenuity to the Industrial Revolution

Human beings have demonstrated remarkable resourcefulness since the dawn of civilization. In ancient times, tools made of stone, bone, and wood were vital for survival, enabling hunting, shelter-building, and agriculture. The development of agriculture itself marked a significant technological milestone, leading to settled societies and the growth of civilizations.

As the centuries unfolded, humanity's inventiveness flourished. Advancements like the invention of writing systems, the wheel, and the printing press revolutionized communication, transportation, and the dissemination of knowledge. However, it was the Industrial Revolution in the 18th and 19th centuries that sparked a technological revolution. Powered by steam engines and mechanization, industries transformed, ushering in a new era of productivity and economic growth.

The Emergence of Electronics and Telecommunications

The late 19th and early 20th centuries witnessed the birth of electronics and telecommunications, laying the groundwork for modern technology. Thomas Edison's invention of the electric light bulb and Alexander Graham Bell's telephone were monumental breakthroughs that revolutionized everyday life.

The early 20th century also saw the development of radio technology, making it possible to transmit information over long distances. This laid the foundation for mass communication and broadcasting. The first half of the 20th century was marked by significant strides in electronics and telecommunications, setting the stage for even more rapid technological progress in the latter half.

The Computer Revolution and the Dawn of the Digital Age

The advent of the computer in the mid-20th century was a defining moment in technological history. The first electronic digital computer, ENIAC, was built during World War II to perform complex calculations for the military. Subsequently, the development of transistors, integrated circuits, and microprocessors paved the way for smaller, more powerful computers.

In the 1970s and 1980s, personal computers entered the scene, transforming the way individuals interacted with technology. The rise of companies like Apple and Microsoft democratized computing, bringing it into homes, schools, and businesses. The computer revolution marked the beginning of the digital age, as digital data and information processing became central to daily life.

The Internet and Global Connectivity

The true turning point in technology came with the invention of the internet. Developed during the late

1960s and early 1970s, the internet initially served as a military communication network. However, its potential for civilian use soon became apparent, and by the 1990s, the internet had become a global phenomenon.

The internet revolutionized communication, commerce, and the exchange of information. Email became a standard form of communication, and the World Wide Web made information accessible to anyone with an internet connection. E-commerce platforms enabled online shopping, transforming retail industries.

The Digital Landscape Today: Mobile Devices, Social Media, and Beyond

As technology continued to evolve, the digital landscape expanded further with the introduction of mobile devices and smartphones. The integration of computers, telecommunication, and internet capabilities into portable devices has profoundly impacted how people access and consume information.

Social media platforms have become integral to modern society, enabling unprecedented levels of global connectivity and communication. Social media has revolutionized how individuals share ideas, express opinions, and participate in public discourse. It has also become a powerful tool for marketing, influencing, and shaping public opinion.

Moreover, the digital landscape has witnessed the rise of cutting-edge technologies like Artificial Intelligence, Virtual Reality, and the Internet of Things. These innovations are transforming industries, from healthcare and education to entertainment and transportation.

Looking to the Future: Embracing Technological Advancements Responsibly

As we stand at the precipice of the future, it is essential to acknowledge the responsibility that comes with shaping the digital landscape. As technology continues to progress at an exponential rate, we must remain vigilant about its ethical use, data privacy, and potential societal impact.

Moreover, ensuring equitable access to technology is crucial to bridge the digital divide and promote inclusivity. The convergence of technology and the digital landscape has the potential to address some of humanity's most pressing challenges, but it also requires thoughtful and responsible navigation.

The historical evolution of technology has been a testament to human curiosity, resilience, and adaptability. From humble beginnings to the digital age, technology has played a transformative role in shaping human civilization. As we embrace the digital landscape of today and the innovations of tomorrow, let us do so with a keen awareness of the ethical considerations and a commitment to harnessing technology for the greater good of humanity.

CHAPTER TWO

Virtual Reality: Where Reality Meets Imagination

In the fast-paced world of technological advancements, Virtual Reality (VR) stands out as one of the most immersive and transformative innovations of our time. With the power to transport us to new realms and experiences, VR blurs the line between reality and imagination. From exploring far-off lands to participating in fantastical adventures, VR opens the door to a world of possibilities that were once confined to the realms of dreams. In this article, we delve into the fascinating world of Virtual Reality, its evolution, and the impact it has on our lives.

Understanding Virtual Reality:

Virtual Reality is a computer-generated simulation of an interactive, three-dimensional environment that can be explored and experienced by an individual using specialized VR equipment. Through a combination of high-resolution displays, motion-tracking sensors, and immersive audio, VR aims to create a sense of presence and complete immersion in a digitally constructed world.

At the core of VR is the concept of "presence" - the feeling of being fully present and engaged in the virtual environment, despite knowing that it is a computer-generated simulation. This sense of presence is what makes VR so compelling and captivating, as it enables users to suspend disbelief and embrace the virtual experience as if it were real.

The Evolution of VR:

The roots of Virtual Reality can be traced back to the 1960s when computer scientists began exploring the concept of simulating environments for research and training purposes. However, it wasn't until the 1990s that VR started gaining mainstream attention, thanks to the development of consumer-grade VR headsets and interactive experiences.

In recent years, significant advancements in technology have propelled VR to new heights. Companies like Oculus, HTC, and Sony have introduced consumer-friendly VR headsets that offer more realistic graphics, enhanced motion tracking, and intuitive controls. As a result, VR has found applications in various industries, from gaming and entertainment to education, healthcare, and even space exploration.

The Power of Imagination:

Virtual Reality's ability to transport users to new worlds and experiences unleashes the power of imagination like never before. In the realm of education, VR is revolutionizing the way students learn by enabling them to visit historical landmarks, explore distant planets, and even interact with long-extinct species. It turns learning into an engaging and unforgettable adventure.

In the world of entertainment, VR has revolutionized gaming, allowing players to step into the shoes of their favorite characters and embark on epic quests.

Beyond gaming, VR has also opened new horizons in storytelling, enabling filmmakers to create immersive, 360-degree narratives that engulf the audience in the story.

Beyond Entertainment: VR for Real-World Applications:

While entertainment remains a significant aspect of VR, its potential goes far beyond just fun and games. In the medical field, VR is being used for simulations and training medical professionals to perform complex surgeries or to treat patients with specific conditions. This technology has proven to be a valuable tool for enhancing medical education and improving patient outcomes.

Moreover, VR has been utilized for exposure therapy, helping individuals overcome fears and phobias by gradually exposing them to their anxieties in a controlled virtual environment. This application of VR has shown promising results in treating conditions such as post-traumatic stress disorder (PTSD), anxiety disorders, and specific phobias.

The Future of Virtual Reality:

As technology continues to evolve, the future of Virtual Reality holds even more promise. With ongoing advancements in hardware, software, and content creation, VR experiences are becoming more realistic, interactive, and accessible. As the technology becomes more widespread and affordable, we can expect VR to find applications in various industries and become an integral part of our daily lives.

Additionally, the convergence of VR with other technologies, such as Artificial Intelligence and haptic feedback systems, will enhance the sense of presence and realism even further. The possibilities for innovation and creativity are endless, and VR is poised to revolutionize the way we learn, work, socialize, and explore the world.

In conclusion, Virtual Reality is a transformative technology that bridges the gap between reality and imagination, offering us thrilling experiences and boundless opportunities for learning and growth. As

VR continues to shape our digital landscape, it is essential to harness its potential responsibly and ethically, ensuring that this exciting technology becomes a force for positive change and enrichment in our lives. With Virtual Reality, the boundaries of what's possible are limited only by our imaginations.

Understanding the Fundamentals of Virtual Reality and Its Applications

Virtual Reality (VR) has emerged as one of the most exciting and transformative technologies of the 21st century. It offers a unique and immersive experience, transporting users to simulated environments and allowing them to interact with digital worlds as if they were real. But what are the fundamentals of Virtual Reality, and how is this groundbreaking technology being applied across various industries? In this article, we will explore the core concepts of VR and its diverse range of applications.

The Building Blocks of Virtual Reality:

At its core, Virtual Reality is an artificial, computer-generated simulation of a 3D environment that can be explored and experienced by an individual. This simulation is created using a combination of cutting-edge hardware and software technologies. The primary components that make up a VR experience are:

Head-Mounted Display (HMD): The VR headset is a crucial element that users wear on their heads to view the virtual environment. The HMD consists of high-resolution displays, often in stereo, which deliver separate images to each eye, creating a 3D effect.

Motion Tracking Sensors: Sensors in the VR headset and sometimes external tracking devices monitor the user's head movements and position in real-time. This tracking ensures that the virtual environment responds accurately to the user's actions.

Audio Output: Immersive sound plays a significant role in creating a sense of presence in the virtual world. 3D spatial audio technology delivers realistic soundscapes that change based on the user's movements and interactions.

Input Devices: To interact with the virtual environment, users require input devices such as handheld controllers, gloves, or even full-body tracking systems. These devices enable users to manipulate objects, navigate, and perform various actions within the virtual space.

Applications of Virtual Reality:

Gaming and Entertainment: Perhaps the most well-known application of VR is in the gaming and entertainment industry. VR gaming allows players to become fully immersed in a virtual world, providing a heightened sense of presence and realism. From action-packed adventures to captivating storytelling experiences, VR gaming has revolutionized how we play and experience video games.

Education and Training: VR has immense potential in education and training. It enables students and professionals to participate in realistic simulations and practice skills in a safe and controlled environment. From medical students performing virtual surgeries to employees undergoing safety training, VR offers an effective and engaging learning experience.

Healthcare and Therapy: In the healthcare sector, VR is being used for various applications, including pain management, physical rehabilitation, and exposure therapy for treating phobias and anxiety disorders. VR simulations allow patients to confront their fears gradually in a controlled setting, leading to therapeutic outcomes.

Architectural Visualization and Design: VR is transforming the way architecture and design are presented and experienced. Architects and designers can create virtual walkthroughs of buildings and environments, providing clients with an immersive understanding of the space before it is built.

Tourism and Virtual Travel: Virtual Reality has opened up new possibilities for the tourism industry by offering virtual tours of destinations, historical landmarks, and cultural sites. Travelers can explore and experience the world from the comfort of their homes, inspiring wanderlust and promoting global understanding.

Social Interaction and Collaboration: Virtual Reality has the potential to revolutionize social interaction by enabling users to meet and interact with others in virtual spaces. VR social platforms and applications offer shared experiences, virtual events, and creative collaboration opportunities.

Space Exploration and Research: VR is being utilized in space exploration for training astronauts and simulating extraterrestrial environments. It also aids scientists in visualizing complex data sets and conducting virtual experiments.

The Future of Virtual Reality:

As technology continues to advance, Virtual Reality is poised to become even more impressive and accessible. Advancements in display technology, haptic feedback, and wireless communication will enhance the sense of presence and realism in VR experiences.

Moreover, as VR becomes more widespread, its integration with other emerging technologies like Artificial Intelligence and Augmented Reality will create even more compelling and innovative applications across various industries.

In conclusion, Virtual Reality has evolved from a niche technology to a powerful tool with a broad range of applications. From gaming and education to healthcare and beyond, VR is reshaping the way we experience the world and interact with digital content. As the technology continues to evolve, the possibilities for VR's impact on society are limitless, making it an exciting frontier for exploration and innovation. As we embrace the potential of Virtual Reality, it is essential to balance technological advancement with ethical considerations to ensure that this revolutionary technology serves as a force for positive change and enrichment in our lives.

Exploring Virtual Worlds, Gaming, and the Potential for Escapism

In a rapidly evolving digital age, the allure of virtual worlds and gaming has captivated millions worldwide. From fantastical realms filled with magical creatures to futuristic landscapes beyond imagination, virtual worlds transport us to places where reality bends and anything becomes possible. Coupled with the interactive nature of gaming, this combination creates a potent cocktail that offers both entertainment and the potential for escapism. In this article, we delve into the fascination of exploring virtual worlds through gaming and the impact it has on individuals and society.

The Allure of Virtual Worlds:

Virtual worlds in gaming provide an opportunity to step out of our everyday lives and venture into realms of endless possibilities. As we don our VR headsets or sit in front of our screens, we embark on journeys where we can be heroes, adventurers, or explorers, each with our own unique story to unfold. These virtual landscapes, meticulously designed and crafted by developers, capture our imaginations, drawing us into their intricately detailed universes.

Beyond the captivating visuals, the allure of virtual worlds lies in the freedom they offer. Players can shape their destinies, make choices, and influence the course of the narrative. These virtual worlds often have their own laws of physics and magic, allowing us to transcend the limitations of reality and experience extraordinary scenarios that would be impossible in the physical world.

Gaming: A Gateway to Escapism:

Escapism is a psychological phenomenon where individuals seek refuge from the stresses and pressures of reality by immersing themselves in alternative experiences. Gaming, especially in virtual worlds, serves as a gateway to escapism, providing a temporary reprieve from real-life challenges.

For some, gaming offers an opportunity to unwind and relax, temporarily disconnecting from the demands of work, school, or personal responsibilities. Stepping into virtual worlds can be a form of stress relief, allowing individuals to recharge and find solace in a world where they have control over their actions and outcomes.

The Potential for Escapism: Balancing Fantasy and Reality:

While the potential for escapism through gaming can be beneficial in moderation, excessive immersion in virtual worlds may have drawbacks. Prolonged escapism can lead to a disconnection from reality and the neglect of real-world responsibilities and relationships. For some individuals, excessive gaming can become addictive, interfering with daily life and social interactions.

As with any form of entertainment, it is essential to strike a balance between indulging in virtual worlds and maintaining a healthy connection with reality. Moderation and self-awareness are crucial in managing the potential for escapism in gaming.

The Positive Impact of Virtual Worlds and Gaming:

Beyond the concerns about escapism, virtual worlds and gaming can have positive impacts on individuals and society. They offer unique opportunities for creativity, problem-solving, and skill development. Many games incorporate intricate puzzles, strategic thinking, and teamwork, fostering cognitive abilities and enhancing critical thinking skills.

Gaming communities also provide a space for social interaction and camaraderie. Multiplayer games and virtual reality experiences enable players to connect with others from around the world, forming friendships and bonds that transcend geographical boundaries.

Additionally, virtual worlds have found applications beyond gaming. From virtual tours of historical landmarks to virtual simulations for educational purposes, these environments can be utilized as powerful tools for learning and exploration.

The Nexus of Imagination and Reality:

The allure of exploring virtual worlds and the potential for escapism through gaming tap into our innate desire for adventure, exploration, and creativity. When experienced in moderation, these virtual landscapes can provide a healthy outlet for relaxation and stress relief.

However, as with any form of entertainment, it is essential to maintain a balance between indulging in virtual escapism and remaining connected to the realities of our lives. By approaching gaming and virtual worlds with mindfulness and self-awareness, we can enjoy the best of both realms—the thrill of exploring virtual landscapes and the richness of the real-world experiences that shape our lives. The nexus of imagination and reality is where we can truly thrive, embracing both the wonders of virtual worlds and the beauty of the world we call home.

CHAPTER THREE

Augmented Reality: Blending Real and Virtual Worlds

In the realm of technological innovations, Augmented Reality (AR) has emerged as a groundbreaking technology that bridges the gap between the physical and digital worlds. Unlike Virtual Reality (VR), which immerses users in a fully computer-generated environment, AR overlays digital information onto the real world, enhancing our perception of reality. From entertainment and education to industry and healthcare, AR is revolutionizing various sectors, opening up a world of possibilities. In this article, we explore the essence of Augmented Reality, its applications, and the impact it has on shaping our daily lives.

Understanding Augmented Reality:

Augmented Reality is a technology that superimposes computer-generated content, such as images, videos, or interactive elements, onto the user's view of the physical world. This fusion of real and virtual elements creates a seamless experience that enhances the user's perception and interaction with the environment.

AR is achieved through specialized devices, such as smartphones, smart glasses, or headsets equipped with cameras and sensors. These devices capture the real-world scene, analyze it, and then overlay digital information in real-time, making it visible to the user.

AR in Entertainment and Gaming:

One of the most well-known applications of AR is in the entertainment and gaming industry. Augmented Reality games, like Pokémon GO, have taken the world by storm, encouraging players to explore the real world while hunting for virtual creatures. These games leverage geolocation and real-world landmarks to create engaging and interactive experiences that blend the virtual and physical worlds.

In addition to gaming, AR is enhancing the entertainment experience through immersive storytelling and interactive marketing campaigns. Companies are using AR to create captivating advertisements, virtual showrooms, and interactive exhibits that capture the attention of consumers in new and innovative ways.

Education and Training with AR:

AR has shown tremendous potential in transforming the field of education and training. By overlaying educational content onto real-world objects and environments, AR enhances learning experiences and increases engagement.

In classrooms, AR can bring static textbooks to life by providing interactive 3D models, historical reenactments, and scientific visualizations. Students can explore complex subjects with greater depth and understanding through interactive learning materials.

Similarly, in professional training settings, AR offers hands-on simulations and real-time guidance. From medical students practicing surgical procedures to industrial workers receiving step-by-step instructions, AR enables more effective and immersive training experiences.

AR in Industry and Commerce:

AR is revolutionizing industries like architecture, manufacturing, and retail. Architects and designers can use AR to visualize and present their designs in real-world settings, allowing clients to experience structures before they are built.

In manufacturing, AR is improving productivity by providing workers with augmented work instructions, assembly guidance, and equipment maintenance support. This leads to more efficient workflows and reduced errors.

For retailers, AR is transforming the shopping experience by offering virtual try-ons for clothing and accessories, interactive product demonstrations, and AR-powered navigation within stores.

Healthcare and Medical Applications:

AR has a significant impact on the healthcare sector as well. Surgeons can benefit from AR overlays during surgeries, displaying vital patient information directly in their field of view, leading to improved precision and efficiency.

AR also plays a role in medical imaging, enabling doctors to visualize 3D models of internal organs and structures, facilitating better diagnosis and treatment planning.

Unlocking New Realities with AR:

Augmented Reality is a transformative technology that blurs the boundaries between the real and virtual worlds. It has the potential to revolutionize entertainment, education, industry, and various other sectors, enriching our daily lives with immersive and interactive experiences.

As AR continues to evolve, it opens up new possibilities for creativity, innovation, and problem-solving. Embracing AR responsibly and ethically will allow us to unlock its full potential, creating a future where the blending of real and virtual worlds enhances our understanding of the world and shapes a new reality of boundless opportunities. Whether it's playing games, learning new skills, or revolutionizing industries, Augmented Reality is transforming the way we interact with technology and the world around us.

Unraveling the Wonders of Augmented Reality and its Integration into Everyday Life

In an era where technological advancements are reshaping the way we experience the world, Augmented Reality (AR) stands out as a remarkable innovation that brings the realms of the physical and digital together. With its ability to overlay virtual elements onto the real world, AR has transcended novelty and become an integral part of our everyday lives. From entertainment and education to retail and communication, AR is unravelling wonders and transforming how we interact with the world around us. In this article, we dive into the captivating world of Augmented Reality, exploring its wonders and the seamless integration into our daily routines.

AR Entertainment: A World of Immersive Experiences:

The entertainment industry has been revolutionized by Augmented Reality, offering a new dimension to our leisure time. AR gaming experiences like Pokémon GO have captured the imagination of millions, encouraging players to explore their surroundings while engaging with virtual elements. The joy of chasing digital creatures through real-world locations exemplifies the seamless integration of AR into everyday life.

Beyond gaming, AR is enhancing the way we experience entertainment content. It allows us to interact with characters from our favorite movies and TV shows, bringing them to life in our living rooms. The integration of AR filters and effects into social media platforms enables us to create fun and engaging content, sparking creativity and connecting with friends in novel ways.

AR in Education: Illuminating Learning Experiences:

AR has become an invaluable tool in the field of education, transforming traditional learning methods into interactive and immersive experiences. In classrooms, students can delve into historical events, explore distant planets, or dissect virtual organisms, all through AR-enhanced educational content. These captivating experiences deepen understanding, enhance retention, and stimulate curiosity.

For remote learning and online education, AR bridges the gap between teachers and students by providing dynamic and engaging learning materials. From interactive 3D models to virtual field trips, AR is making education accessible, exciting, and effective for learners of all ages.

AR in Retail and Commerce: A Revolution in Shopping:

The retail industry has undergone a significant transformation with the integration of Augmented Reality. AR-powered shopping experiences allow customers to virtually try on clothing, accessories, and cosmetics, eliminating the need for physical fitting rooms and providing a personalized shopping experience.

In the realm of interior design and home improvement, AR enables customers to visualize furniture and decor in their homes before making a purchase. This allows for informed decisions and reduces the likelihood of returns, enhancing customer satisfaction.

AR in Communication and Collaboration: Bringing People Closer:

AR is reshaping the way we communicate and connect with others. AR-powered communication platforms allow users to share and interact with virtual objects and information during video calls, making remote collaboration more engaging and productive.

In social settings, AR filters and effects add an element of fun and creativity to our conversations, making virtual interactions feel more personal and entertaining.

AR in Navigation and Exploration: Navigating the World with Ease:

AR is transforming how we navigate and explore our surroundings. AR navigation apps overlay directions and real-time information onto the user's view of the world, simplifying the process of finding locations and points of interest.

For travelers, AR-powered city guides offer an immersive way to explore new places, providing historical information, reviews, and interesting facts as users walk through the city streets.

Conclusion: Augmented Reality: A Seamless Part of Our Lives

The wonders of Augmented Reality are evident in its seamless integration into everyday life. As technology continues to advance, AR is becoming more accessible and versatile, offering a multitude of benefits across various industries.

From entertainment and education to retail and communication, AR has proven its potential to enhance our experiences and interactions with the world. As we embrace this captivating technology, it is essential to continue exploring its possibilities responsibly and ethically, ensuring that AR enriches our lives while respecting our privacy and maintaining a balance between the real and digital realms.

In the years to come, Augmented Reality will undoubtedly unravel even more wonders, transforming how we live, learn, and connect in ways we could only imagine. With AR as a seamless part of our daily lives, the future is filled with boundless opportunities, blending the physical and digital worlds into a harmonious tapestry of innovation and wonder.

Examining AR's Impact on Industries such as Education, Healthcare, and Entertainment

Augmented Reality (AR) has proven to be a transformative technology, reshaping various industries and unlocking new possibilities for innovation and engagement. From education and healthcare to entertainment, AR has made a profound impact on how we learn, heal, and immerse ourselves in captivating experiences. In this article, we will examine the remarkable impact of Augmented Reality on industries such as education, healthcare, and entertainment, and explore the exciting prospects it holds for the future.

AR in Education: Enhancing Learning Experiences

AR has revolutionized the landscape of education, enriching learning experiences and engaging students in interactive and immersive ways. Traditional textbooks have been complemented or replaced by AR-enhanced materials, offering dynamic 3D models, interactive simulations, and virtual field trips.

With AR, students can explore historical events as if they were present, examine complex scientific concepts up close, and interact with virtual artifacts from various cultures and periods. This hands-on approach to learning fosters deeper understanding, improves retention, and sparks curiosity among learners.

Moreover, AR has expanded access to education beyond traditional classrooms. Online courses and virtual classrooms leverage AR to create engaging learning environments that bridge the gap between students and instructors, regardless of geographical distance. The democratization of education through AR has the potential to revolutionize global learning opportunities.

AR in Healthcare: Transforming Medical Practice

In the healthcare industry, AR is transforming medical practice, training, and patient care. Surgeons can use AR to overlay vital information, such as patient data, imaging, and navigation aids, directly onto their field of view during surgeries. This real-time visual guidance enhances precision, reduces errors, and improves patient outcomes.

For medical training, AR offers immersive simulations that allow aspiring medical professionals to practice procedures and gain valuable hands-on experience in a risk-free environment. From surgical simulations to medical diagnostics, AR is redefining medical education and skill development.

AR also plays a critical role in patient care and therapy. It enables healthcare providers to display diagnostic information and treatment plans directly to patients, enhancing communication and shared decision-making. Additionally, AR-based therapy interventions help patients with rehabilitation, pain management, and mental health conditions.

AR in Entertainment: Redefining Immersive Experiences

Entertainment is another industry profoundly impacted by AR, offering audiences immersive experiences that blur the line between reality and imagination. AR-powered gaming experiences have captured the world's attention, with games like Pokémon GO and Harry Potter: Wizards Unite becoming global phenomena.

Beyond gaming, AR has opened up new possibilities in storytelling, offering interactive and personalized narratives. Immersive theater experiences and AR-powered performances bring characters and scenes to life, engaging audiences in entirely novel ways.

The integration of AR into the entertainment industry has also revolutionized marketing and advertising. Brands leverage AR filters and experiences on social media to create captivating campaigns that engage consumers and strengthen brand connections.

The Future of AR: Limitless Opportunities

As AR technology continues to evolve, its potential impact on industries is boundless. We can expect further advancements in AR hardware, making it more accessible and user-friendly. Additionally, the convergence of AR with other emerging technologies like Artificial Intelligence and 5G will unlock even more exciting applications.

In the education sector, AR will continue to evolve as a powerful tool for personalized and adaptive learning experiences. AR will find increased applications in specialized training, such as professional development, emergency response, and industrial skills training.

In healthcare, AR will further enhance medical practice, telemedicine, and patient care, paving the way for augmented surgeries, remote medical consultations, and augmented reality-powered medical devices.

In entertainment, we can anticipate more innovative AR experiences, blurring the boundaries between virtual and physical worlds. From interactive concerts to mixed reality theme parks, AR will redefine how we engage with entertainment content.

Embracing the Augmented Reality Revolution

Augmented Reality has emerged as a transformative force across industries, unleashing a wave of innovation and creativity. In education, healthcare, and entertainment, AR has demonstrated its ability to enrich experiences, drive engagement, and elevate human potential.

As we embrace the Augmented Reality revolution, it is essential to do so responsibly and ethically, safeguarding user privacy and ensuring equitable access to these transformative technologies. By harnessing the power of AR in education, healthcare, and entertainment, we can create a future where learning is limitless, healing is advanced, and entertainment is a boundless journey into the realm of imagination. The impact of AR on these industries is just the beginning, and the potential for a more augmented and enriched world is limitless.

CHAPTER FOUR

Artificial Intelligence: The Brainpower Behind the Curtain

Artificial Intelligence (AI) is no longer a distant dream of science fiction; it has become an integral part of our modern world, driving innovation and reshaping industries across the globe. As the brainpower behind the curtain, AI systems process vast amounts of data, analyze patterns, and make informed decisions, transforming the way we live, work, and interact with technology. In this article, we explore the essence of Artificial Intelligence, its applications, and the profound impact it has on shaping our present and future.

Understanding Artificial Intelligence:

At its core, Artificial Intelligence refers to the ability of machines or computer systems to perform tasks that typically require human intelligence. These tasks include learning from experience, recognizing patterns, understanding natural language, and making decisions based on data.

AI can be classified into two broad categories: Narrow AI and General AI. Narrow AI, also known as Weak AI, is designed to perform specific tasks, such as virtual assistants, recommendation systems, and image recognition. On the other hand, General AI, also known as Strong AI, would possess human-like cognitive abilities and the capacity to understand and perform any intellectual task that a human can.

AI Applications in Various Industries:

AI has found applications in a wide range of industries, transforming processes, and revolutionizing traditional practices. Some notable applications include:

Healthcare: AI is revolutionizing healthcare with its ability to analyze vast amounts of medical data and assist in diagnostics, personalized treatment plans, and drug discovery. AI-powered medical imaging systems can detect diseases with greater accuracy, while AI chatbots provide patients with personalized health advice.

Finance: In the finance industry, AI is driving innovations in fraud detection, algorithmic trading, and customer service. AI-powered robo-advisors provide personalized investment recommendations, making wealth management more accessible and efficient.

Education: AI is reshaping education with personalized learning platforms that adapt to individual student needs and abilities. Intelligent tutoring systems provide tailored support and feedback, enhancing the learning experience.

Manufacturing: AI-powered robots and automation systems are improving efficiency and precision in manufacturing processes. Predictive maintenance powered by AI algorithms helps avoid equipment failures, reducing downtime and costs

Transportation: AI is driving advancements in autonomous vehicles and smart transportation systems, paving the way for safer and more efficient travel.

Entertainment: AI algorithms are used in the entertainment industry to personalize content recommendations on streaming platforms and create realistic virtual characters and environments in movies and video games.

Machine Learning: The Heart of AI

At the core of AI's capabilities lies the concept of Machine Learning (ML). Machine Learning is a subset of AI that allows systems to learn from data and improve their performance over time without being explicitly programmed. ML algorithms identify patterns in data, make predictions, and adapt their behavior based on feedback, enabling AI systems to become more accurate and efficient with experience.

Supervised learning, unsupervised learning, and reinforcement learning are common types of Machine Learning, each with its unique approach to training AI models.

The Ethics of Artificial Intelligence:

With the increasing integration of AI into various aspects of our lives, ethical considerations have become paramount. Issues such as bias in algorithms, data privacy, and the impact of automation on jobs raise critical questions about responsible AI development and deployment.

AI developers, policymakers, and society as a whole must work together to ensure that AI technologies are developed ethically, with transparency, fairness, and accountability as guiding principles.

Unleashing the Power of Artificial Intelligence

Artificial Intelligence is a driving force behind the curtain of the digital revolution, bringing about a new era of innovation and progress. As AI continues to advance, it has the potential to unlock solutions to some of humanity's most pressing challenges, from healthcare and climate change to education and beyond.

As we venture further into the world of AI, it is crucial to embrace its potential responsibly, guided by ethical principles that prioritize the welfare of humanity. By harnessing the brainpower of Artificial Intelligence, we can unleash a future where technology empowers us, enriches our lives, and propels us towards a more intelligent and inclusive world. The journey of AI has only just begun, and the wonders it holds for humanity are yet to be fully revealed.

Demystifying Artificial Intelligence and Machine Learning

Artificial Intelligence (AI) and Machine Learning (ML) have become buzzwords in today's tech-driven world, but their complexity can often leave people feeling mystified and unsure of what they truly mean. In this article, we aim to demystify AI and ML, providing a clear understanding of these transformative technologies and their real-world applications.

What is Artificial Intelligence?

At its core, Artificial Intelligence refers to the simulation of human intelligence in machines that are programmed to think and perform tasks like humans. The goal of AI is to enable machines to learn from experience, adapt to new inputs, and perform tasks that would typically require human intelligence. AI encompasses a broad spectrum of technologies, ranging from basic rule-based systems to advanced machine learning algorithms.

Machine Learning: A Subset of AI

Machine Learning is a subset of Artificial Intelligence that focuses on developing algorithms and statistical models that enable computers to learn from data without being explicitly programmed. In other words, ML systems improve their performance on a specific task as they are exposed to more data. Instead of following fixed instructions, these algorithms use patterns and trends within the data to make predictions, classifications, and decisions.

Supervised Learning, Unsupervised Learning, and Reinforcement Learning

Machine Learning can be classified into three main types:

Supervised Learning: In supervised learning, the algorithm is trained on labeled data, where each input has a corresponding output. The goal is for the model to learn the mapping between inputs and outputs, making accurate predictions on new, unseen data.

Unsupervised Learning: Unsupervised learning involves training the algorithm on unlabeled data, allowing it to find patterns and structures within the data. This type of learning is useful for tasks like clustering and anomaly detection.

Reinforcement Learning: Reinforcement learning is a different approach, where an agent interacts with an environment and learns by receiving feedback in the form of rewards or penalties based on its actions. The goal is for the agent to find the best actions to maximize cumulative rewards over time.

Real-World Applications of AI and ML:

AI and ML have permeated various industries, transforming the way we live, work, and interact with technology. Some real-world applications include:

Natural Language Processing (NLP): AI-powered NLP enables machines to understand, interpret, and generate human language. Virtual assistants like Siri and Alexa use NLP to respond to voice commands and engage in conversations.

Image and Speech Recognition: ML algorithms can analyze and identify patterns in images and audio, enabling applications like facial recognition, self-driving cars, and voice assistants.

.

.

Recommendation Systems: AI-driven recommendation engines suggest products, movies, or content based on user preferences, enhancing user experiences on platforms like Amazon and Netflix.

Medical Diagnosis: AI and ML are used to analyze medical data, assist in disease diagnosis, and predict patient outcomes, leading to more accurate and timely medical interventions.

Financial Services: AI-driven algorithms are used in fraud detection, credit scoring, and trading to improve security and efficiency in financial transactions.

Ethical Considerations:

As AI and ML continue to play a more significant role in society, ethical considerations become crucial. Issues like bias in algorithms, data privacy, and the potential impact on jobs require careful examination and responsible development.

Transparent and accountable AI practices, along with clear regulations and guidelines, are essential to ensure that these technologies benefit humanity ethically and responsibly.

Understanding AI and ML for a Better Future

Demystifying Artificial Intelligence and Machine Learning is vital for us to grasp their potential and implications accurately. As these transformative technologies become more integrated into our lives, understanding their applications and impact empowers us to make informed decisions and contribute to shaping a future where AI and ML create positive outcomes.

By embracing AI and ML responsibly, we can unlock a world of possibilities, where intelligent machines complement human capabilities, solve complex problems, and enhance our overall quality of life. As we navigate the ever-evolving landscape of AI and ML, the key lies in harnessing these technologies to create a brighter and more inclusive future for all.

Analyzing AI's Influence on Decision-Making, Automation, and Ethics

Artificial Intelligence (AI) has emerged as a powerful force, reshaping the way we make decisions, automate processes, and confront ethical challenges in various domains. As AI systems become more sophisticated and widespread, it is essential to examine their impact on decision-making, automation, and the ethical considerations that arise. In this article, we delve into the nuances of AI's influence on these critical aspects of our lives and explore the implications for society.

AI in Decision-Making: Enhancing Insights and Accuracy

AI's ability to process vast amounts of data and identify patterns enables it to augment human decision-making processes significantly. In fields such as finance, healthcare, and business, AI-powered analytics provide valuable insights that support better decision-making.

In finance, AI algorithms analyze market trends, historical data, and economic indicators to make informed investment decisions. This enhances the accuracy and efficiency of portfolio management, leading to more successful investment strategies.

In healthcare, AI assists in diagnosing medical conditions by analyzing patient data and medical images. AI-driven diagnostic tools can detect diseases with high precision, leading to earlier detection and timely treatment.

In business, AI-powered data analytics help organizations make data-driven decisions, optimize processes, and identify growth opportunities. AI algorithms can forecast market trends, customer preferences, and supply chain fluctuations, aiding businesses in staying ahead of the competition.

AI and Automation: Revolutionizing Industries

Automation is one of the most visible impacts of AI, revolutionizing industries by streamlining processes and increasing efficiency. AI-powered robots and software automate repetitive tasks that were once performed by humans, freeing up valuable time and resources.

In manufacturing, AI-driven robots perform tasks with precision and speed, reducing errors and increasing production capacity. Automated assembly lines significantly enhance productivity and reduce production costs.

In customer service, chatbots and virtual assistants powered by AI handle customer inquiries and support, providing quick responses and 24/7 availability. This automation improves customer experiences and reduces the workload on human agents.

In transportation, AI-driven self-driving cars and autonomous drones have the potential to revolutionize mobility and logistics, improving safety and efficiency.

Ethical Considerations in AI: Ensuring Responsible Development

As AI becomes more prevalent, ethical considerations become paramount. AI systems can perpetuate biases present in training data, leading to biased decision-making and discriminatory outcomes. Ethical concerns also arise in areas like data privacy, autonomous weapons, and AI's impact on employment.

To ensure responsible AI development, it is crucial for developers, policymakers, and society at large to address these ethical challenges proactively. Transparency, fairness, and accountability should guide AI implementation to avoid unintended consequences and to build trust among users.

Embracing AI for a Positive Future

AI's influence on decision-making, automation, and ethics is undeniably transformative. By augmenting human decision-making, automating repetitive tasks, and optimizing various industries, AI holds the promise of creating a more efficient and advanced society.

However, as we embrace AI's potential, it is vital to strike a balance between progress and ethical considerations. Responsible AI development, transparency in algorithms, and ongoing monitoring are essential to ensure that AI serves the greater good without infringing on privacy, perpetuating biases, or compromising human values.

As AI continues to evolve, collaboration between stakeholders is critical to shaping its trajectory for a positive and inclusive future. By harnessing the power of AI responsibly, we can unlock its full potential and use it as a force for positive change in our increasingly interconnected world. With a clear focus on ethical principles and a commitment to responsible implementation, AI can become a transformative tool that enriches our lives and enhances our collective well-being.

CHAPTER FIVE

Digital Art and Creativity: A Canvas Without Boundaries

In the ever-evolving digital age, technology has unleashed a new realm of artistic expression and creativity known as digital art. As traditional tools merge with cutting-edge technologies, artists have gained access to a vast digital canvas without boundaries, redefining the way art is created, experienced, and shared. In this article, we explore the fascinating world of digital art and its transformative impact on the artistic landscape.

What is Digital Art?

Digital art encompasses a wide range of artistic practices that utilize digital technology as a fundamental part of the creative process. It goes beyond simply using digital tools for traditional art forms; it explores new frontiers where technology is not just a medium but an integral part of the artistic expression.

Digital art can take various forms, including digital painting, computer-generated art, digital photography, multimedia installations, interactive art, virtual reality experiences, and more. The key element is that digital technology serves as a crucial element in the creation and presentation of the artwork.

The Advantages of Digital Art: A World of Creativity

Digital art offers artists a world of creative possibilities and advantages:

Flexibility and Experimentation: Digital tools allow artists to experiment freely, easily undo mistakes, and try multiple variations without the constraints of traditional mediums. This fosters exploration and enables artists to push the boundaries of their creativity.

Endless Tools and Effects: Digital software offers an array of tools, brushes, and effects that empower artists to create intricate and unique artworks. From realistic textures to fantastical effects, digital artists have a vast toolbox at their disposal.

Efficiency and Productivity: Digital art streamlines the creative process, allowing artists to work efficiently and make changes quickly. This can lead to increased productivity and faster iterations of ideas.

Collaboration and Accessibility: Digital art has facilitated collaboration between artists worldwide. Artists can share their work online, collaborate on projects remotely, and engage with a global audience with ease.

Digital Art in Contemporary Art Movements:

Digital art has become an integral part of contemporary art movements, pushing the boundaries of what is considered art. From the early experiments of pixel art to the rise of digital installations and immersive experiences, digital art has found its place in the art world.

Digital Art Challenges and Ethical Considerations:

As digital art blurs the line between reality and virtuality, it raises new challenges and ethical considerations. Issues like copyright infringement, authenticity, and the impact of technology on the art market have come to the forefront.

Ensuring the proper attribution and protection of digital artworks poses unique challenges, as digital files can be easily copied and shared. Additionally, questions of ownership and authenticity arise when artworks exist as digital files that can be duplicated indefinitely.

Digital Art and Audience Engagement:

One of the most exciting aspects of digital art is its ability to engage audiences in innovative and interactive ways. Digital installations, augmented reality experiences, and virtual reality artworks invite viewers to be active participants in the art, blurring the lines between the artist, artwork, and audience.

These interactive experiences offer a new dimension to the artistic encounter, encouraging viewers to explore, interact, and be immersed in the artwork. Digital art challenges the traditional notion of a passive audience and transforms viewers into co-creators of the artistic experience.

Embracing the Boundless Canvas of Digital Art

Digital art has shattered the confines of traditional artistic expression, opening up a boundless canvas of creativity and innovation. With digital tools and technology as their ally, artists explore uncharted territories, pushing the limits of their imagination and redefining what is possible in art.

As digital art continues to evolve, it is essential for artists, audiences, and the art community to embrace this transformative medium with an open mind. Embracing the boundless canvas of digital art allows us to explore new dimensions of creativity, interactivity, and collaboration. The fusion of technology and artistic expression brings us closer to a future where art knows no boundaries, and the possibilities for creative expression are limited only by our imagination.

Delving into the Realm of Digital Art, Animation, and Design

In the age of technology and boundless creativity, the realm of digital art, animation, and design has emerged as a captivating world of limitless possibilities. From digital illustrations that transport us to fantastical landscapes to animated characters that come to life on our screens, this realm has redefined the way we perceive and interact with visual arts. In this article, we embark on a journey into the captivating realm of digital art, animation, and design, exploring the tools, techniques, and impact of these transformative mediums.

Digital Art: Where Imagination Meets Technology

Digital art represents the convergence of traditional artistic skills and cutting-edge technology. It encompasses various forms, including digital painting, 3D modeling, photo manipulation, and graphic design. Artists harness the power of digital tools, such as graphics tablets, stylus pens, and sophisticated software, to create intricate and visually stunning masterpieces.

Digital art offers artists a wide range of creative possibilities and advantages. It allows for easy experimentation, enabling artists to explore different styles and techniques without the fear of making permanent mistakes. Digital software provides an extensive array of brushes, textures, and effects, empowering artists to express their imagination with unparalleled precision and detail.

One of the most intriguing aspects of digital art is its ability to blend different artistic mediums seamlessly. Traditional painting can be merged with photography, and hand-drawn elements can be incorporated into digital collages. This fusion of techniques results in breathtaking works of art that transcend the boundaries of individual artistic disciplines.

The Magic of Animation: Bringing Art to Life

Animation is the art of bringing static images to life through the illusion of movement. In the realm of digital animation, artists harness technology to create dynamic characters, scenes, and stories that captivate audiences of all ages.

From classic 2D animations to cutting-edge 3D CGI (Computer-Generated Imagery), animation has evolved significantly over the years. 2D animations evoke a sense of nostalgia, with their hand-drawn charm and fluid motion. On the other hand, 3D CGI delivers stunning visual realism and immersive experiences that transport audiences to vibrant virtual worlds.

Animation has become a powerful medium for storytelling, not just in films and television but also in video games, advertising, and educational content. It allows for the depiction of complex narratives, emotions, and fantastical scenarios that may be difficult or impossible to recreate in live-action formats.

Digital Design: Crafting Visual Experiences

Digital design is a versatile realm that encompasses various creative disciplines, including graphic design, user interface (UI) design, and web design. Designers leverage digital tools to craft visually appealing and functional experiences across digital platforms.

In graphic design, artists create eye-catching visuals for branding, marketing materials, and advertisements. Digital graphics can be easily adapted for different mediums, making them essential components of modern marketing campaigns.

UI design focuses on creating user-friendly and visually appealing interfaces for websites and applications. Intuitive navigation, well-organized layouts, and aesthetically pleasing elements enhance user experiences and engagement.

Web design brings together artistry and technology to create stunning websites that capture the essence of brands and businesses. Responsive design ensures seamless experiences across various devices, enhancing accessibility and user satisfaction.

Impact on Creativity and Expression

The realm of digital art, animation, and design has revolutionized the way artists express themselves and communicate with audiences. Digital tools have democratized art creation, making it accessible to a broader range of artists worldwide. The ease of sharing digital artworks online enables artists to connect with global audiences and receive instant feedback on their creations.

Moreover, the interactivity and dynamic nature of digital art and animation have enhanced audience engagement. Users can interact with digital artworks, exploring hidden details, and immersing themselves in captivating narratives. This interactive element bridges the gap between the artist's vision and the viewer's experience, fostering a deeper connection between creator and audience.

A Flourishing Realm of Endless Creativity

The realm of digital art, animation, and design continues to flourish and evolve, captivating audiences and empowering artists worldwide. It stands at the crossroads of human imagination and technological innovation, transforming traditional art forms into awe-inspiring digital masterpieces.

As technology advances, so will the possibilities for creative expression in this realm. With each new development, digital artists and animators will continue to redefine the boundaries of visual storytelling, leaving us spellbound with their ingenuity and artistry.

Embracing the realm of digital art, animation, and design allows us to immerse ourselves in a world where imagination knows no bounds and creativity has the power to transport us to places we could only dream of. This boundless realm beckons us to explore, create, and celebrate the ever-unfolding magic of digital artistic expression.

Showcasing Innovative Works and Artists Who Push the Boundaries of Creativity

In the dynamic and ever-evolving world of art, there are visionary artists who constantly challenge the limits of creativity, redefining artistic expression and inspiring awe with their innovative works. These artists fearlessly explore new mediums, blend diverse disciplines, and push the boundaries of traditional art forms. In this article, we showcase some of these trailblazers who captivate audiences and leave an indelible mark on the art world.

1. Yayoi Kusama - Infinity Mirrors of the Mind:

Renowned Japanese artist Yayoi Kusama is celebrated for her mesmerizing Infinity Mirror Rooms, immersive installations that transport viewers into a realm of infinite reflections. By employing mirrors, lights, and polka-dot patterns, Kusama creates kaleidoscopic environments that evoke a sense of wonder and infinity. Her art encourages introspection and contemplation, making the observer an integral part of the artwork.

2. Banksy - Provocative Street Art:

Banksy, the elusive and enigmatic street artist, challenges conventional norms and societal constructs through his provocative and politically charged works. With stencils and spray paint as his tools, Banksy's creations address issues of social injustice, political corruption, and the human condition. His art has the power to provoke thought and ignite conversations, as it emerges unexpectedly on urban walls around the world.

3. Olafur Eliasson - Art of the Senses:

Danish-Icelandic artist Olafur Eliasson is renowned for his captivating installations that engage the senses and immerse viewers in multisensory experiences. Eliasson often incorporates natural elements such as light, water, and air to create immersive environments that blur the lines between art, architecture, and nature. Through his art, he invites audiences to explore the interplay of perception and reality.

4. Cai Guo-Qiang - Explosive Creativity:

Chinese contemporary artist Cai Guo-Qiang brings a unique twist to artistic expression by using gunpowder and fireworks as his medium. His explosive artworks, often created on large canvases, are a harmonious blend of chance and control, as he orchestrates the fiery spectacle. Cai's art explores themes of cultural exchange, environmental issues, and the transient nature of existence.

5. Marina Abramović - Performance Art as a Medium:

Serbian performance artist Marina Abramović is renowned for her daring and emotionally charged performances that challenge the limits of the human body and psyche. Her art delves into themes of vulnerability, endurance, and the connection between artist and audience. Abramović's performances are transformative experiences, transcending traditional art forms and pushing the boundaries of what art can be.

6. Studio Drift - The Intersection of Art and Technology:

Studio Drift, a Dutch art collective, merges art, design, and technology to create awe-inspiring and interactive installations. Their works often incorporate elements of kinetics and robotics, allowing sculptures to move and respond to the environment and viewers. Through their art, Studio Drift explores themes of nature, human behavior, and the impact of technology on our lives.

Pioneers of Creativity

The artists mentioned above are just a few examples of the visionary creators who push the boundaries of creativity, fearlessly exploring uncharted territories in the world of art. Their innovative works inspire and challenge us to perceive art in new ways, provoking introspection and sparking conversations about the human experience and our place in the world.

As technology, society, and culture continue to evolve, so will the realm of artistic expression. These pioneering artists remind us that creativity knows no limits, and art will always find new avenues to captivate, provoke, and inspire. They leave us with a